JACQUELINE HARDIN-GAUTIER

Stolen Identity Restored

How His Love Pursued Me

P139

To God, my everything—You are my truth, my hope, my strength, my inspiration, and my keeper. Your love envelops me, guiding my every step and illuminating the path of my life, encapsulating me in Your power and Your Glory, Submerging me in Your essence. In moments of joy and sorrow, You are still my absolute everything. You have remained my steadfast anchor, and my most High and Secret place. I am found secure in You, and forever and always my affections belong to You alone.

"For we are God's masterpiece. He has created us anew in Christ Jesus, so we can do the good things he planned for us long ago."

— Ephesians 2:10 (NLT)

Contents

Preface

In a world where identities are often shaped by circumstances, relationships, and the weight of our pasts that is soaked in the environment that we have been born into, A Stolen Identity Restored: How His Love Pursued Me offers a powerful reminder that our true value is not defined, and identified by our struggles, and who we are doesn't have to be tied to where we have come from in this earth, but the love that seeks to redeem us has defined who we are. Jocelyn's story is a testimony to the glorious transformative power of discovering one's true identity in Jesus Christ.

As you pull up a front-row seat to Jocelyn's life unfolding, you will witness a raw and unfiltered glimpse of her reality and travel a path of pain and destruction transformed by hope—a life marked by many challenges that some turning the pages may find difficult to comprehend. From the grip of addiction to the scars of abuse and the mentality of criminality, her experiences reflect a harsh truth: that this world and its environment can strip us of our identity and leave us completely unrecognized, until hope awakens. This beautiful narrative is a remarkable tale of the restorative power that comes from embracing one's identity in Christ.

Discovering that God had already planned and chosen her in Christ Jesus before she was ever known to her parents, and that she was truly loved and accepted in Him, empowered Jocelyn to break free from the chains of her past. She realized that her true history was always rooted in Christ Jesus. This irrevocable love of God calls Jocelyn back into her rightful position in Jesus.

In these pages, you will find not just a story of personal triumph, but an invitation to reflect on your own journey toward uncovering your identity in Christ. The power that comes from acknowledging our true identity can liberate us from the burdens we carry, enabling us to fully step in and embrace the lives we were always intended to walk in.

This is your initiation into the powerful revelation of a Stolen Identity Restored. Grab hold of your seatbelt and buckle in for the ride, as we are pursued together by the incredible truth of God's love for His creation. Explore the reality of your identity in Jesus. Fully embrace your inheritance, which can only be accessed when you recognize and authenticate who you truly are. Receive your identity today.

Acknowledgments

To my father, William Hardin, a man of strength and resilience:

You are truly my best friend outside of my husband. Though you have not always been an easy man, you have been the best man for me. You have been a constant presence in my life, never allowing me to succumb to weakness. While we may not always see eye to eye, you remain one of my biggest support systems, especially in my later years.

I am forever grateful for your tough love, which has instilled in me invaluable lessons about standing tall and never shrinking back in the face of opposition. You have taught me the significance of perseverance. Your open arms have always welcomed me, reminding me that love truly prevails.

By never shying away from the hard truths of life, you have equipped me to navigate turbulent moments with greater confidence. Thank you for being the incredible father that you are.

To my mother, Dena Hardin, who has passed on but remains a cherished presence in my heart. Eventually in life grew to become more than my mother but a true confidante and showed me what it truly means to be pursued by love. Once you found sobriety, your unwavering pursuit of me is a true testimony to the power of redemption and unconditional love. Your story of redemption in your own life continues to inspire me, and I carry the lessons of your love with me always.

To my grandmother, Lonnie Hardin, who taught me the importance of the name of Jesus. Your faith and wisdom have left an indelible mark on my heart, guiding me through many of life's challenges.

To my aunt, Jacqueline Hardin, who took me to my first little white church, where I met Jesus for my self the first time. Your nurturing spirit opened the door to my walk of faith, and I am forever grateful for that foundational experience.

I would like to say something to my aunt Willette Thornton, who ignored all the darkness that tried to surround me, and in her sweet silence welcomed me to engage with God in one of the most confusing times in my life. I am forever grateful.

To my stepmother, Cheryl Evans, in a world often filled with indifference, where right and wrong can seem blurry, you have been a steadfast guide, teaching me to always strive to do the right thing, regardless of what others may choose. Thank you for being a moral compass when I did not have one of my own.

When my mother was not a constant presence in my life, you stepped in with open arms, loving me as if I were your own. Your kindness and support have made such a great impact on my life and my character, and I am truly grateful for the love and wisdom you've shared.

To my husband, Ricardo Gautier, I need to say so much more to you. You are my bestest of bestest friends, my sounding board, and my support system—truly an expression of God's love toward me as a husband and a kinsman redeemer. You are the place I go when I need support.

It doesn't go unnoticed how he believes in me, encourages me, pushes me, exhorts me, trusts me, and fortifies me. I am completely in love with you.

You are my greatest supporter and companion, whose faith in me inspires me to soar beyond my limits. Your encouragement fuels my passion, and I am so grateful to do life with you.

To my children, Marion Hardin, Earl Harris III, and Serenity Hardin, your love has given me the courage to walk a different path. May I always exemplify the values of love, strength, and perseverance, so you may grow up knowing the beauty of faith and the power of hope. To my grandchildren, Thraxtin Hardin, Hope Harris, and Earl Harris IV, you are a source of joy that enriches my life in ways I cannot express.

And to Apostle Zoe, whose guidance has been transformative in my life—thank you for opening my eyes to my true identity in Christ. Your wisdom and unwavering faith have illuminated a path for me that I can only pave forward on, I bless God for you helping me embrace the fullness of who I am meant to be. Your teachings have instilled in me a deep understanding of my position in Christ and God's original intent for me. I have newfound confidence in myself because I now understand that the fullness of Christ is in me, expressing Himself through me.

To Alexis Shabazz, who is always pushing me to be a steady writer, never giving up on my craft, I thank God for your friendship and encouragement.

To Shari Twine, thank you for challenging my views and ideas; you have been an invaluable asset in my writing, even when you may not have realized it.

To all my friends who have been my spiritual guides, your support and encouragement have enriched my journey, reminding me that I am surrounded by love and community.

As you read these pages, I hope you find inspiration to reflect on your own life and the relationships that have shaped you. Each of us has a story to tell, and it is my hope that this book encourages you to embrace yours with courage and authenticity.

Thank you for joining me on this journey of discovering our identity in Christ Jesus.

Prologue

The God of all creation has a plan for everyone and everything. The command of His words is like a pen in His hand, tracing and laying the foundation of all that exists in creation and in every detail of our lives. Through Him, all things were made, and without Him, nothing has been made (John 1:3, TPT). Nature reveals the works of His hands.

"Now ask the animals, and let them teach you; ask the birds of the air, and let them tell you; speak to the earth, and it will teach you; let the fish of the sea declare this truth to you. Who among all these does not recognize that the hand of the Lord has done this?" (Job 12:7–9, NKJV).

He is the Creator of the universe, and its grandeur testifies to Him as its Maker and Sustainer. He is El Roi, "The God who sees" (Genesis 16:13, TPT). He sees you in every aspect of your being, including the deepest places of your heart shaped by your experiences. He loves you with an everlasting love and draws you to Himself with unfailing kindness (Jeremiah 31:3, TPT), summoning you back to the blueprint of who He created you to be before the fall, back to the unstained innocence in which you were made even before He laid the foundation of the universe (Ephesians 1:4, TPT).

It is always the Father's heart to bring His creation back to Himself so that we may discover the overflow of His fullness meant to dwell within us, allowing us to be identified with Him

(Colossians 2:10, TPT).

His eyes have seen everything from the beginning to the end of time—everything that has happened and everything that will unfold. He created you and knows you intimately (Isaiah 44:24, TPT). He knows your name, the exact moment you entered the world, and every detail of your life—how you think, how you speak, and why you dance to your own tune (Isaiah 43:1, TPT; Psalm 139:16, TPT). He understands the depths of your character because He intricately formed your innermost being (Psalm 139:13-14). He knows your precise location, both physically, spiritually, and emotionally; He is aware of your condition, position, and stature (Psalm 139:1-5, 13-16, TPT).

In all of His knowing, God is fully aware of who the world around you has told you that you are, shaped by your experiences, your nature, and how you were nurtured. He understands what you have been defined as as a result of these things. But He is also the author, and designer of who you are really meant to be, He is the crafts maker of your original workmanship—He created the manual that entails who He created you to be, made in His image and likeness (Genesis 1:27, TPT). Through every challenge and twist in life, Yahweh is continually drawing you back to your intended design—the purpose you were meant to fulfill before you entered through the womb of your mother into the shaping of sin and iniquity brought on by the Fall of mankind (Psalm 51:5, TPT).

Just as He molded Adam from the dirt, your life may sometimes feel shaped by the messy, broken pieces of your experiences. Yet, Elohim had a plan for Adam—a plan to take all the dirty places of his formation and transform them into something beautiful.

He breathed the fullness of Himself into Adam, authenticating him and making him whole—a living soul. This same intention is at work in you! With every road, with its ups and downs, God's long-range plan is to draw you back to a place in Him—the One who formed you (Ephesians 1:9-10, TPT).

Even though God knows your name, you can be a casualty of being a Jane or John Doe until you are introduced to the author of your life. The world, or the environment around you, with all its trials and distractions, often steals your identity and perverts the truth of who you are meant to be by convincing you that you are the sum of your experiences in life. Until one is identified, we wander, disconnected from the truth of who we are meant to be. It is only when we accept the summons, drawing us to the appointed introduction in time, and restoring His identity within us, that we are truly recognized and can walk in the fullness of who we were designed to become.

A Reflection on Identity

Understand that Yahweh knew what He was getting into when He made you. You are His creation, molded with a specific purpose. Every masterpiece undergoes a process of formation and shaping, and you are a masterpiece in His hands (Ephesians 2:10, TPT). Some steps in this process may be painful for both the creation and the Creator.

Our God, who is omniscient, knows where you came from, what you have been through, and what you are living through right now. He sees and knows the moments when you have felt consumed by darkness, completely void, without form, and lost. But darkness is not dark to Him (Psalm 139:12, TPT). He knows your exact location, even in the darkness, so even when you feel lost and unidentified, hidden beneath all that you think you have become, you can find yourself if you search for Him.

Even in the midst of this darkness, the process of creation can

3

indeed be ugly, broken, and messy. Yet, Yahweh knows every detail from the end to the beginning and is fully aware of what is needed to guide you back to your intended design. Know this: nothing in your life was ever meant by Elohim to harm you; rather, He is powerfully able to use every experience for your good to draw you back to your place in Him—before the fallen state, before the experiences and the nature around you stole your identity (Romans 8:28, TPT).

The Journey Back to Yourself

But trust me when I tell you this: when you locate Him—I mean when you truly locate Him—He will bring you back to yourself. He will bring you back to where you were meant to be from creation. He will bring you back to Himself, which is your true self, your Christ self, your identified self. When He created you in His image and likeness, the Bible says that He gave you the ability to reflect Him on this earth in the very essence of all that you are, to dominate, to rule, and to be a force of light that overshadows all darkness (Genesis 1:26-28, TPT; Matthew 5:14-16, TPT; John 8:12, TPT).

He is the God who hovers over the darkest places and commands light! While the earth was still in complete darkness, without form and void, the Spirit of God hovered over that darkness and displayed His majesty at the great clockwork that introduced His wonder and might. As He spoke, the very sound of His voice commanded light and fullness in the earth (Genesis 1:1-24, TPT).

Just as God was present in Genesis 1, calling forth His purpose in the hidden treasures and the chaotic void laid up in the darkness of the earth, He is also present in the roll call of your life, bringing order to all the messy, broken circumstances and calling you forth into your destined position, into the light. Since

He is omnipresent, He knows about the scars and the wounds that tried to leave you formless. He knows the exact location of those scars, the precise location of the incision that left you vulnerable. Because He is aware of these exact locations, He is also the only one with the vast ability to heal you (Jeremiah 30:17, TPT). In fact, if you are a born-again believer, then you are already healed by His stripes! All you have to do is accept your healing.

Healing and Restoration

God is not only present in your life; if you have accepted your identity as His child, then He is also present inside of you. Since you are created in His likeness, your voice carries the same vibration in the earth to command the light to overtake any darkness that has tried to overcome you or anything in your atmosphere. Not only do you have the ability to accept your healing, but you can also heal thy own self because the Physician lives in you!

I know that life can tell quite a different story. In the tapestry of our lives, wounds and scars can seem etched into our souls by the harsh realities we have faced. These wounds come in many forms—the searing pain of mental, physical, and sexual abuse, the haunting echoes of rejection, abandonment, and neglect, and the crushing weight of betrayal and violation.

From the innocent child who has suffered the unspeakable horrors of molestation to the grown woman or man who bears the scars of rape, from the college student who was drugged and violated to the individual who has endured the relentless cycle of verbal, physical, or emotional abuse at the hands of those meant to protect and love them, these wounds run deep. They cut through the very fabric of our being, leaving us feeling unworthy, rejected, abandoned, unloved, unreachable, forsaken, broken, and ugly. They leave us unidentified.

These circumstances have been set as traps, aimed at stealing your true identity—the essence of who God says you are. They seek to bury you under pain and convince you to identify with what has happened to you. Yet, the moment you receive your true, authenticated identity in Christ, you become dead to your old self and fully alive in Him, free from everything that once tried to hold you back.

Embracing Your True Identity

In the unfolding narrative of life, where the echoes of despair attempt to overthrow you, I encourage you to seek your summoning to an identity in Christ. As the unidentified becomes identified in Jesus, hope will surely emerge as a triumphant force. This dominion and power in Christ Jesus will dethrone and overtake all that has ever tried to entrap you. You will be empowered by the understanding of the astonishing height, depth, and width of the extravagant love of God (Ephesians 3:18-19, TPT).

However, we must also come to terms with the fact that there is another presence—an unwanted intruder—lurking in the darkness, wielding pain and despair as weapons forged for our destruction. This is the lie of inadequacy, the one that has tried to strip us of our true identity. This adversary, an enemy of God, spins lies to sow seeds of shame, erode dignity, and foster self-doubt, attempting to convince you that you are worthless or less than. But where darkness lurks, God's light overtakes it; darkness cannot diminish the light (John 1:5, TPT).

Though adversaries may wage war against you (1 Peter 5:8, TPT), be of good courage, for God, the ultimate warrior, goes with you. He is waiting for you to let Him fully express Himself through you. Remember the true nature of the battle: "It is not against flesh and blood but against spiritual forces of evil in the heavenly realms" (Ephesians 6:12, TPT). However, their power has been rendered useless for those who have found themselves in Christ Jesus; your victory is assured by the triumph of Jesus (Colossians 2:15, TPT).

As you navigate life's challenges, stay sober-minded and alert to the spiritual realities at play. Understand that if you secure yourself in Christ Jesus, you can bring order to the chaos, for the Creator, Sustainer, and Fulfiller of all things lives in you. When He has full expression, nothing can defeat you.

So, as you turn through the pages of Jocelyn's story, and indeed, through the chapters of your own life, remember this: God's purpose always prevails. As His love pursues you, take a seat in His endless love, bow out gracefully to the power of the Almighty God, and let Him rise up inside of you as you identify yourself as a champion in every battle, finding your identity in Christ Jesus, seated in heavenly places, far above all the principalities, powers, and rulers of dark places (Ephesians 1:20-21, TPT).

Introduction

"For our struggle is not against flesh and blood but against the rulers, against the authorities, against the powers of this dark world, and against the spiritual forces of evil in the heavenly realms" (Ephesians 6:12, NIV).

If you pay close attention, you'll see that this is the structure of an army prepared for war. In every war, there are casualties, and sometimes prisoners are taken. Most wars are fought with many battles, often over territory. The enemy, Satan, wants to take all the territory he can, especially the hearts and minds of individuals. He uses people to fight his battles, to spread darkness and extend his evil forces over the land. While this battle rages in the spiritual realm, we experience its effects on earth. It manifests in flesh and blood, generation after generation, in lives pulled into captivity.

But God, in His power and mercy, has stepped into the situation to free His beloved from the grip of the enemy if you decide to accept His invitation into your identified life in Christ Jesus!

The Battle Begins: Washington's Story

Jocelyn's story begins in one of these battles—one where her father, Washington, became a casualty of the enemy's plan to steal, kill, and destroy. Washington was a jack of many trades: a mechanic, a taxi driver, and an ambulance worker. Anything he put his mind to, he excelled at. But this battle met him not in his work, but as a drug dealer and gang member, trying to survive the streets of Detroit. He was raised in a community entrenched in this spiritual warfare, where boys like him were at war with their own flesh, driven by the LOVE of money and the possessions it promised.

"But those who crave the wealth of this world slip into spiritual snares. They become trapped by the troubles that come through their foolish and harmful desires, driven by greed and drowning in their own sinful pleasures. And they take others down with them into their corruption and eventual destruction. LOVING money is a root of all evils. Some people run after it so much that they have given up their faith. Craving more money pushes them away from the faith into error, compounding misery in their lives!" (1 Timothy 6:9-10, TPT).

The spiritual forces of evil sought to capture souls by first stripping away their identities. This tactic, as old as warfare itself, involves breaking the will of captives. Just as ancient captors stripped individuals of their identity—removing names, culture, and heritage to mold them into instruments for a foreign power—the enemy targeted Washington in a similar manner. His true identity was stolen before he even recognized it. The enemy exploited his surroundings—the streets, the allure of quick money, and the false respect of a drug dealer—to distract him from discovering who he really was. By keeping Washington focused on counterfeit success, the enemy aimed to prevent him from realizing his misidentification in this world.

The Shaping of Identity

Washington's original design had been shaped by God when he was knit together in his mother's womb (Psalm 139:13, TPT). But the moment he was born, something else entered the picture—in iniquity (Psalm 51:5, TPT), a force that sought to alter his God-given identity. It was as though a virus had been introduced into his spiritual makeup, distorting the DNA God had placed in him. Much like a biological virus, which invades healthy cells, reprograms them with false information, and spreads through the body to cause dysfunction, this is exactly how iniquity had worked in Washington's life to corrupt his perception of who he truly was. This virus of sin caused him to miss the mark of who he truly was and set out to alter his spiritual design, influencing how he saw the world and himself.

Much like Achan in the book of Joshua, whose greed for silver and gold led to destruction for his entire community (Joshua 7), Washington's desire for wealth brought ruin not only to himself but also to those around him. Achan missed the mark, causing Israel to lose the battle at Ai and bringing God's anger upon the people. Similarly, Washington's pursuit of money and power came at a high price. The drugs he sold didn't just affect strangers—they tore apart his own home. His wife, Delta, became one of the casualties of this war, falling victim to the very drugs Washington dealt. This coveting after what money could provide was destroying his family from the inside out, creating a ripple effect that spread throughout his community.

Despite being raised in a loving, stable home with Christian values, Washington was lured into becoming a soldier on the frontlines of darkness. His parents gave him everything they could—strong values, private school, and integrity—but somehow the environment he was surrounded by still was able to sneak in and corrupt his identity. The enemy planted seeds of deception in Washington's environment, influencing him to identify with what he saw on the streets, blinding him to the truth of what and who God had actually created him to be. God had a purpose for Washington: to be in His image and likeness!

The Illusion of Success

The gold chains, cars, and lifestyle he sought were spoils of a spiritual war, things devoted to destruction, just like the treasures Achan coveted. Washington thought he was making choices to survive, to provide for his family, but in reality, God was ready to overwhelm him with every form of grace so that he would have more than enough of everything—every moment and in every way—to make him overflow with abundance in every good thing he would find himself doing (2 Corinthians 9:8, TPT).

But Washington didn't understand that this was his portion, so instead, he became a captive in this spiritual war. Washington's identity was hidden under the rubble of the world around him. He was living as a prisoner, caged by a false perception of himself and everything around him, unaware that the very things he was chasing were keeping him bound in spiritual captivity and causing him to miss the mark.

Hope in the Darkness

But there is hope even in the darkest of battles. Isaiah 61 speaks of the good news that God is still setting captives free. The truth is that He already set you free when Jesus came back for you over 2,000 years ago. He is just waiting on you to walk out of the prison that He has already made a way for you to come out of. He is still calling for you to walk out of the dark place into His kingdom of light and receive the identification that was restored to you through Jesus Christ.

Washington, though he couldn't see it at the time, was not

beyond the reach of God's voice that echoes into darkness and commands light. Even darkness had to obey the call to let there be light. In the same way, we have to obey God and choose the light over the darkness so that we can gleam in and see who we were always meant to be, and lean into the image of God.

No matter how far we go, God is always reaching out for His beloved, drawing us back to Himself and to the identity He designed for us in His likeness (Romans 5:8, TPT; 5:10, TPT). God continually summons us to receive our identity as sons and daughters of God. This is why He sent Jesus—to reconcile and restore us, even while we were still far from Him, to restore the genetic code and to reverse the virus. Jesus is the antidote to restore this stolen identity.

Psalm 139:13-14 (TPT) says, "You made all the delicate inner parts of my body and knit me together in my mother's womb. Thank you for making me so wonderfully complex! Your workmanship is marvelous; how well I know it."

These words beautifully describe God's intricate design of each person—wonderful, complex, and marvelous. None of us are a mistake, worthless, discardable, or forsaken. God, the Creator of the universe, crafted us long before the world ever saw us (Jeremiah 1:5, TPT).

Consider the works of famous artists like Picasso, whose paintings have sold for over $100 million. Yet, you were created by God, the most exquisite artist ever known, with the most vast collection of art imaginable. He holds the most valuable pieces known to mankind and is the One who owns everything— the whole earth and all who live in it (Psalm 24:1, TPT). He created the vast universe and all its grandeur (Genesis 1:1, TPT), and each of His creations—including you—is worth more than all the money in the world (Matthew 6:26, TPT). There is no number that can fully describe how valuable you are to Him. He knows your full potential and worth, having crafted not only your outward appearance but also every delicate detail within you (Luke 12:7, TPT). God knows the full appraisal of His work, and He appraised you as priceless.

There may be times in your life when you've felt unseen, unheard, undervalued, or rejected by the world around you. People often fail to recognize the potential within others because they misidentify them—like a valuable piece of art mistaken for something of less value, similar to a forger altering an original piece of artwork, degrading its appearance to hide its true value. The forger's goal is to keep the art's worth hidden, because if the real identity were discovered, the piece of art would shine and testify to how majestic the Artist actually is. Similarly, when people look at you through the distorted lens of their biases, experiences, or the world's standards, they fail to see the divine potential that God, the One who created you, has placed within you (Genesis 1:27, TPT). They only see the flaws the forger has put there to misidentify you.

Misidentification happens when people judge you based on surface appearances—your past mistakes or current struggles (John 7:24, TPT). They fail to recognize who crafted you and what God has called you to be. Like treasure buried beneath dirt, your true worth may be hidden by circumstances, but that doesn't change the reality of your identity. People assign labels based on their limited understanding, but these labels are far removed from the identity God has given you. He has identified you as His (Isaiah 43:1, TPT). While others may misjudge you, God knows the masterpiece He created in you, waiting to be revealed (Ephesians 2:10, TPT).

Sadly, people do misidentify you—sometimes even those

closest to you. Family, friends, and those you trust can often see you through the wrong lens (Mark 6:4, TPT). For Jocelyn, this misperception came from her mother, Delta, and for Delta, it stemmed from her own mother, Gladys. While God was knitting Jocelyn together, creating His marvelous workmanship and crafting every curve, mark, distinction, and detail, her mother envisioned her as something less, as if Jocelyn had no value. Remember that no matter what experiences Jocelyn goes through, she has immense value—and so do you, for you have been crafted by the greatest artist in the world.

1

Mamma Don't Want No Black Baby

On a scorching May day, Delta's words cut through the air of the hospital room like a sharp blade: "I don't want a black baby," she uttered, her voice heavy with prejudice and fear. Delta's words weren't just about Jocelyn's skin color—they reflected her own distorted view of herself and the world. She had internalized society's biases and allowed them to cloud her ability to see her own child's God-given beauty.

Washington felt the sting of those words, not just because they rejected their daughter, but because they rejected the essence of who Jocelyn was created to be. To Washington, her deep skin tone reflected the diversity of colors in the Creator's pen and was a testament to the beauty of God's creation. However, Delta, blinded by her own insecurities, couldn't recognize the tapestry of God's craftsmanship in her daughter.

Identity is more than what we see on the surface; it's rooted in the truth that we were made by God, for God, and in His likeness. When people misidentify you—whether through prejudice, bias, or ignorance—it's often because they fail to strip away the outer layers to uncover the truth of who you really are. As a result, they may start to place labels on you. If you aren't careful, you might begin to believe these false labels and misidentify yourself. But God, the One who created you and knows you intimately (Jeremiah 1:5, TPT), understands your true worth. He designed you with a divine purpose, and He is waiting for you to embrace this truth.

The reality of who you are in God's eyes can never be changed. He sees you as His marvelous workmanship, wonderfully and fearfully made (Psalm 139:13-14, TPT), regardless of how the world chooses to see you (1 John 3:1, TPT). This is why it is so important to look to God, the One who created you and knows you intimately (Jeremiah 1:5, TPT), for your identity. Only He can give you the genetic key through Jesus Christ to unlock your true self (John 6:44, TPT; Galatians 2:20, TPT). His truth will pull you away from the false perceptions and labels that others' words and actions may have placed on you. The truth is that you are wanted by God, and there is no better sense of belonging than to know that you are wanted and belong to God, the Creator of all the universe and everything in it, the One who holds it all together, the One who was before the beginning, who is eternal, and the very source of life itself. He wants you, and you are chosen by Him, and that is the only perception that matters. He has made an opportunity and a way for you to step in and accept the fact that He has called you to Himself as His beloved child.

MAMMA DON'T WANT NO BLACK BABY

2

El Roi Sees You

When someone doesn't know who another person is and the unique value they carry, they likely misjudge even their own purpose and worth. This misjudgment is rooted in a distorted view of God and the world around us (2 Corinthians 4:4, TPT). This is one of the tools that the enemy uses to try to confuse us about who God is! Such a distorted perspective leads to mishandling creation—not just the world around us, but we mishandle ourselves.

The world refuses to identify God. As a result, it doesn't understand the purpose of His creation (Colossians 1:16, TPT). Blinded by the darkness, unable to perceive the beauty in each person as God's masterpiece, intricately woven with purpose (Ephesians 2:10, TPT).

What was meant to reflect the glory of God is often overlooked, misjudged, and undervalued, leaving the masterpiece of God's design unseen (Isaiah 43:7, TPT). Misidentification leads to the mishandling of people, thwarting their God-given identity and reducing them to something they were never meant to be (Romans 8:19, TPT).

Consider a musical instrument, like a violin. If a violin is misused—played without care or without understanding of its craftsmanship—it creates dissonance instead of harmony (1 Corinthians 12:14-18, TPT). Worse, if handled too roughly, it can break, losing its ability to produce beautiful music. Likewise, when people are misjudged or mistreated, and mishandled because of a distorted view, the unique design and value of that person can become damaged (Matthew 10:29-31, TPT). Even if this has been your story, you have got to get God's perspective, and grab hold of the truth that the One who designed you—can repair any kind of damage(Jeremiah 30:17, NIV).

El Roi, "the God who sees," knows everything (Genesis 16:13, TPT). He sees you even when the world around you makes you feel invisible or misidentifies you. He understands your struggles and has the remedy to restore you. In fact, He has already sent restoration for you through His Word, revealed in a man who is also God—His name is Jesus, the Christ, the Messiah, the Savior, and the Restorer of the world (1 Peter 5:10, TPT; John 1, TPT).

God has already seen you as identified in Jesus because He has completed the work to bring you back to Himself. This is His perspective concerning you: to Him, you are a finished work, created in Christ Jesus before the foundation of the world (Ephesians 2:10, NIV). He is simply waiting for His creation to adopt His perspective—a God perspective that allows us to recognize the beauty in each person as God's workmanship, even when the world refuses to acknowledge it. That is why it is imperative that we adopt a God perspective instead of the world's perspective.

* * *

Consider Hagar, an Egyptian slave in Abraham's household (Genesis 16:1-16, TPT). During Hagar's time in the ancient Near Eastern world, a woman's value was often tied to her fertility, and slavery was an accepted part of life. Hagar found herself at the heart of a conflict not of her making (Genesis 16:2, TPT).

Hagar had been taken from her homeland to serve in a foreign household. Although the biblical text doesn't detail her journey to Abraham and Sarah's encampment, it's likely she was given as part of a diplomatic exchange or purchased during their stay in Egypt (Genesis 12:10-20, TPT). Regardless, she had no choice; she entered a world where her identity was defined by servitude, and her autonomy was limited by her status as a slave (Exodus 21:20-21, TPT).

God had made a promise to Sarah and Abraham regarding a child (Genesis 15:4-5, TPT), but as time passed without fulfillment, Sarah's faith began to waver under the relentless pressure of a society that judged a woman's worth by her ability to bear children (Genesis 16:1, TPT). Her barrenness likely became a source of personal anguish and public shame. In her desperation, Sarah devised a plan: she would use her Egyptian slave, Hagar, to bear her child.

Do you see how the labels we and the world place on ourselves can distort our self-perception? Sarah couldn't see Hagar for who she was; she only saw what she lacked, reducing Hagar to a means of fulfilling her void. As a slave, Hagar had no agency over her body or future, thrust into the role of surrogate (Genesis 16:3-4, TPT). However, once Hagar conceived, a shift occurred—she looked upon Sarah with contempt. The Hebrew word qalal means "to make light of" or "to consider insignificant." Hagar no longer viewed Sarah as significant, feeling her pregnancy elevated her status. This change created deep tension in the household.

Sarah, burdened by years of unfulfilled longing for a child, found Hagar's contempt unbearable. The very woman she had given to bear Abraham's child now looked down on her! This situation likely fueled Sarah's frustration—Hagar's attitude was painful and seemed to reject the social order that provided stability and respect in her home.

On the other hand, Hagar felt alone, identified solely as a slave girl, unaware of her true identity and the immense value she carried (Genesis 16:5-6, TPT). Likely feeling misused, abused, and confused, she fled. Isn't that what pain often compels us to do when we don't understand our identity or purpose, especially in moments of despair?

So, Hagar ran into the desert (Genesis 16:6-7, TPT). In that desolate place, the Bible tells us the angel of the Lord found her—not only did He find her, but He identified her by name, "Hagar," rather than the label "Egyptian slave girl." God didn't call her what others had labeled her; He called her by her name (Genesis 16:7-8, TPT). Although she felt alone, overlooked by society, she was not forgotten by her Maker. He pursued her with love during the most desperate moment of her life. He saw her pain and promised her a son named Ishmael, meaning "God hears," a constant reminder of His intimate awareness of her situation and involvement in her future. She was identified and located by the God who sees and hears (Genesis 16:11, TPT).

It is in the realization that you have been pursued by God and that He knows you by name where your true identity awakens. When you become aware of who you truly are and your purpose is defined, the labels, marks, and brands the world has tried to impose on you can no longer dictate your identity. This is a transformative labor, giving birth to something beautiful, as you adopt a new perspective—a God perspective.

3

Distorted Identity

The enemy meant to break Delta. It was an unknown foe, hidden in the shadows, working against her, forming weapons of destruction that aimed to shatter her life. Remember the principalities and powers in dark places; these were the unseen forces used to diminish her sense of worth and distort her understanding of what she was really made for, much like Hagar.

But this battle against Delta's identity didn't begin with her—it was woven into her story long before she was born. Her mother, Gladys, had lived with her own distorted sense of identity, shaped by the brokenness and rejection she endured. That brokenness, like a shadow, stretched into Delta's life. When someone grows up with pain, rejection, and a distorted view of themselves, they often unknowingly pass that hurt down to the next generation (Exodus 20:5, TPT).

It's important to remember that this distortion of identity was never God's plan. When God created us, He said, "Let us make them in our image, after our likeness" (Genesis 1:26, TPT). This was a declaration of our purpose—to reflect God's image, carrying His likeness, and living out a divine purpose (Ephesians

2:10, TPT). Our true identity was always meant to mirror His nature, full of love, power, and purpose.

Just like DNA holds the blueprint for every cell in our bodies, God's Word holds the blueprint for who we are meant to be (1 Peter 1:23, TPT). His likeness is embedded in us from creation, but when trauma, rejection, or sin enters our lives, it distorts that divine DNA, altering the way we see ourselves and others. That's exactly what the enemy wants: to confuse and distort the image of God within us (John 10:10, TPT).

Delta wasn't a victim of her circumstances—she was a victim of a stolen identity, because hers had been altered by the pain. When the weight of trauma, rejection, and brokenness is placed on someone, it doesn't just affect their mind; it distorts the way they see everything.

If Delta and Hagar were friends, they could have been each other's support. Hagar might have told Delta that all this suffering would not be in vain, that what others used for evil, God would use for good (Genesis 50:20, TPT). I wish Hagar could have told Delta that El Roi sees her, that she is valued, and that she is not forsaken (Isaiah 43:1, TPT).

Delta's troubles started because her mother's picker for a good man was broken when she and Delta were abandoned by Delta's biological father, James. After he left, Gladys settled down with Wallace and had more daughters, but despite Wallace's love, the void was too deep for Gladys to fill. Eventually, she married a man named Ernest, hoping he could fill the emptiness. But Ernest wasn't the kind of man you bring home to your little girls. While Gladys was out trying to bury her own pain, Delta and her sisters were receiving wounds of their own, and pain that would not easily be mended. They were preyed upon by Ernest; he tore away at their sense of innocence and stripped them of their identity before they were old enough to even know what an identity even was.

With every touch, he tore at their value, leaving them empty, just as Gladys had felt. Ernest's vile actions left Delta emotionally distant, forcing her to hide her feelings within deep walls of darkness. Jocelyn always wondered why Delta seemed cold and emotionally unavailable. Abuse like this can bury a person in such a deep, dark hole that finding the light again seems impossible (Isaiah 9:2, TPT). But what is impossible with man is possible with God (Luke 18:27, TPT). Remember in Genesis, darkness was over the face of the deep, yet God's light spoke into that void, bringing life and order.

Though the enemy sought to steal Delta's identity, distorting her vision of who she was by burying her in pain, there is a preset that God has placed within us—one that mirrors His image and likeness. This divine imprint is designed to draw us back to our reflection of Him, overcoming the forces of darkness that seek to distort our perception of ourselves. The principalities and powers in dark places may aim to keep our identity captive, but God's light breaks through the deepest shadows, reclaiming and restoring who we are meant to be in Him. Know this: Jesus came to set the captives free. All you have to do now is walk out of the prison.

The wonderful thing is that although life's pain can cause a distortion, when we come into contact with our true birthplace by meeting Jesus—the One who came and destroyed the very power of death (Hebrews 2:14, TPT)—our identification is restored back to us. Jesus becomes our passport to get back to who we've always been since the beginning of time (Ephesians 1:4, TPT). All you have to do is find out who Jesus is (John 14:6, TPT). When you do, your identity will no longer be distorted but completely restored (2 Corinthians 5:17, TPT). And if you already understand who you are, take a moment to thank God for your status as a child of God. Let the undeniable implications of this truth permeate every aspect of your being as you reflect on the information on your original identification card, recognizing your completeness in Christ Jesus (Colossians 2:10, TPT). This restored location in a persons being is where God is desiring to draw Delta to.

4

Lost Identity

Washington and Delta had been friends for most of their child-hood, with Delta often hanging out with Washington and his sister. Delta was known for her tough, carefree attitude, while Washington, despite knowing her troubled past, found himself drawn to her hardness. Over the years, they each had children—Washington with Candice had a son named Kenshaw, and Delta with another man had a daughter named Shanice—but they remained friends. Washington's father always felt Delta was bad news and tried to keep them from an intimate relationship, but eventually, Washington and Delta married.

After their marriage, Delta and Washington had three ad-ditional children together: Delmont, Jocelyn, and Jamal, all born while Delta was on drugs. Washington was aware of her struggles, from popping pills in middle school to her escalating addiction, yet he couldn't resist her. Delta seemed easier to get along with when they were high together, but as more children arrived, Washington began to realize that things had to change. When Jocelyn was born and Delta disappeared for months, Washington knew he had to stop selling drugs.

Even as they welcomed Jamal, Washington's youngest son together, into the world, Delta's addiction continued to pull her away, leaving Washington to grapple with the reality of their situation. He tried to do right by pursuing a legitimate career as an ambulance driver and learning his father's trade as a mechanic. However, Delta's addiction persisted, and Washington found himself giving in to her desires just to keep her around. Eventually, when he couldn't meet her needs, she would leave again.

Their destructive choices stemmed from a deep misunderstanding of their true selves, rooted in an environment that acted like a virus, fracturing their identities and corrupting their perceptions of who they were meant to be. This environment convinced them of a false identity, distorting their understanding of self-worth and purpose. They were living out shattered identities, passed down like a curse from generation to generation. Delta's fractured sense of self, caused by the abuse she endured as a child, had warped her perception of the world and herself.

Life had left her cold and detached. Unable to see her own value, she struggled to recognize the worth of her children. The lies she believed about herself were so deeply ingrained that they colored her perspective on everything, including her role as a mother. The drugs became an escape, obscuring the shattered truth of who she really was—a woman created in the image of God, coded with inherent value and purpose.

Washington faced an identity crisis as well. Despite his attempts to do right, he was constantly drawn back into the lie that he needed more than one woman to be fulfilled. The streets fed him a deceptive image of masculinity that lured him away from the strength he could have drawn from his father, leading him down a path far removed from his true potential. In this struggle, he had somehow grabbed hold of someone else's identification card, believing it to be his own. If he had possessed the right one—the one that held the demographics of how to embrace the identifying factors that had been sketched into his DNA from the beginning of time—he might have found his true self. Yet, the truth of who he was, buried beneath the world's lies, was calling him out of darkness. He only needed to listen.

Every time Washington chased other women or Delta slipped deeper into her addiction, they were searching for something—anything—that could fill the voids of their fractured identities. Their toxic lifestyle wasn't just a series of bad decisions—it was the result of a deep, inherited distortion of their identity. The sad truth is that Delta and Washington were unintentionally teaching their children the same destructive patterns to which they had become accustomed. Although Washington was trapped in a different kind of identity crisis, constantly searching for validation in the streets, in women, and in everything but the one place where his true identity could be found—in God.

As the years went on, the cycle continued. Delta would leave for her lover called addiction, and Washington would seek his value in the attention from other women. But despite their unfaithfulness to each other, Washington always waited for Delta to come back. In his heart, he believed that what they had was love. Yet the Bible describes love very differently: "Love is patient, love is kind. It does not envy, it does not boast, it is not proud. It does not dishonor others, it is not self-seeking, it is not easily angered, it keeps no record of wrongs" (1 Corinthians 13:4-5, TPT). What Washington and Delta had wasn't love—it was a reflection of the brokenness they felt inside.

Washington and Delta's children were growing up in an

environment where their value was obscured, just like their parents. But deep down, Washington knew there had to be more. His "God self" was buried beneath the weight of the lies he had believed about needing more than one woman, about needing to prove his worth.

The only way to break these cycles was for them to recognize what God said about them; instead, they succumbed to what the world around them had defined them to be. The truth was that they didn't need the streets, or the drugs, or the approval of others to be whole. They had been created with purpose and value, and their true worth could only be found by re-registering themselves at the DMV of heaven, where they could get the demographics about the true intent of their identity.

5

Seeds of Truth

Washington stood alone in the hallway, his heart heavy as he glanced back at his children and his wife, Delta. He had made up his mind—he couldn't live like this any longer. Delta was slipping further into addiction, and their home had become a battlefield. Leaving tore at his soul, but staying felt like an even greater betrayal to himself, Delta, and his children. He walked out the door, tears streaming, believing his departure was the only way to make his family whole. As he journeyed south to Georgia, guilt weighed on him. He was determined to salvage what was left of his family, even if it meant starting over without them.

Louetta and Albert, Washington's parents, lived downstairs and helped raise his children. Louetta had a gift for seeing past people's mistakes, loving them through their brokenness, while Albert, more stern and pragmatic, took care of the practicalities. Together, they stepped in after Washington left, and when Delta would disappear, ensuring that the children were cared for. Louetta, deeply rooted in her faith, knew that there was an enemy, and she understood that this enemy's strategy was a plan to destroy her children's and grandchildren's identities.

In the midst of all the turmoil and raging storms, Louetta believed that the truth of God's design for their lives was stronger than any lie and any strategy that the enemy could forge. She knew that God's DNA—the divine nature He imprinted on them when He created them in His image—was still in them, waiting to be claimed.

Every night, Louetta prayed with her grandchildren, teaching them the Lord's Prayer (Matthew 6:9-13, TPT) and ensuring they understood that when they prayed, they should pray in the name of Jesus (John 14:13-14, TPT). It was important to her to instill an understanding of the power of Jesus and His name in their hearts. She recognized the spiritual battle they were in for and knew the storm was coming. But she was laying their foundation on the rock of Jesus (Matthew 7:24-25, TPT), trusting that one day the truth of their identity in Christ would break through the lies that had been whispered over their lives.

She held on to the hope that one day they would grasp the truth of who they were meant to be, and these timeless truths would push past the contamination of their environment and the lies of the enemy. She set out to create an alternative environment for them. In Psalm 91, she told them to apply it to their memory because, when they found themselves with destruction and chaos all around them, they could find themselves in this world but, at the same time, in the shelter of the Lord. In this shelter, they could find protection.

Jocelyn would listen to her grandmother and think about all the chaos surrounding her—everything she had no control over. She would wonder how she could get to this shelter that Louetta talked about; it sounded like a place of peace, and she wanted to learn how to get there.

* * *

Everything had become calm for a short while. Delta had disappeared, and Delmont, Jocelyn, and Jamal were safely stable and being cared for by their grandparents. It was a tranquil moment, but this peace was fleeting, as the storm named Delta was looming on the horizon, ready to sweep in like a flood and threaten the fragile stability they had found with their grandparents.

She had emerged from one of her infamous binges with the intention of doing the right thing and being present for her kids. However, just as always, the calm at the center of the storm was merely a prelude, waiting for the right amount of heat to stir the winds into action. A buried fear was on the verge of being triggered, and with it, the storm would rage once again.

It all started when Delmont came in, dragging Jocelyn into the house, his voice loud with accusation. "Mamma, Jocelyn's been nasty under the neighbor's house!" Delta turned to see Jocelyn standing there, her dress soiled and her face a mixture of confusion and fear. In that moment, Delta's heart stopped. She saw more than just a dirty dress—she saw her past, her own innocence stolen night after night, with shame buried deep inside.

Fear and panic surged through her as she grabbed Jocelyn's hand. "What happened?" she demanded, her voice trembling. "Why are you so filthy? What were you doing?" Jocelyn stood silent, unable to explain, the word "filthy" burning inside her like a brand. Her mother's fear twisted into anger, and instead of listening, Delta lashed out, threatening Jocelyn if she ever did something like this again.

What Delta didn't know was that Jocelyn had been under

the house with Monte, the oldest son of a family friend. He had grabbed her and frightened her into silence, and though she couldn't remember exactly what had happened, she knew something wasn't right. But in that moment, Delta's own pain overshadowed her daughter's, and the cycle of unspoken facts of life continued.

Later that night, fear of the unknown began to settle in Delta's chest—a fear of what Jocelyn might have experienced, something she didn't think she could handle the answers to. She buried the urge to ask because it was too unbearable to imagine. In this moment, she pushed aside all the racing, tormenting thoughts of what might have been as she gathered all four of her children in bed with her. Quietly, she prayed a simple childhood prayer over them, her voice barely above a whisper but loud enough for Jocelyn to hear:

"Now I lay me down to sleep, I pray to the Lord my soul to keep. If I should die before I wake, I pray the Lord my soul to take."

It was a small gesture, a flicker of hope in the darkness. Despite everything, there was still something deep inside Delta that understood that God was the only source to make what was broken whole. Yet, just as her own mother had failed her, she was failing to listen to her daughter's cry for help. But the seeds of truth that Louetta had planted were still there in the darkness, making strong roots that would one day bear beautiful fruit.

Even when pain, confusion, and chaos are stirring all around you, the genetic code hosting your identity screams its truth even louder; God's origin story for you is stronger. His blueprint lies dormant in the deep, undiscovered places within, waiting to be awakened.

This truth, this long-range plan of God—this great mystery

He implemented from the beginning of time—holds an unfailing purpose for Jocelyn and is sure to be fulfilled (Ephesians 1:9-10, TPT). The foundation of Jesus that Louetta had built for her grandchildren had no choice but to produce life, with every seed of the truth of Jesus Christ that she had instilled being part of the groundwork for establishing the destiny and purpose that God would surely accomplish in them (Ephesians 1:11, TPT).

6

A Spark in The Darkness

Jocelyn felt the sting of what seemed like a mother's neglect, like a song that had gradually faded into silence, leaving her with only hollow notes that distorted her understanding of what a mother's love should truly be. She had tried to speak up, to make her mother see the pain she was feeling, but her words were swallowed by the chaos of Delta's tsunami of emotions. It felt as though Jocelyn didn't matter, that she was invisible in her mother's world. Yet, even in the midst of the hurt, Jocelyn held onto a small spark of hope. The previous night, she had heard her mother quietly pray. It was a flicker of light in the overwhelming darkness that the storm had caused, and it made Jocelyn believe that maybe, just maybe, her mother could still find her way back.

Delta, on the other hand, was drowning in her own storm. Her mind raced with fears about her children's future, and sleepless nights turned into endless anxiety. Though she tried to be present—engaging in daily routines and making an effort to connect with her children—the weight of her addiction, triggered by the sight of Jocelyn's stained dress, pulled her back into old patterns. Just as these patterns sought to distort her perception of her purpose as a mother, with thoughts from the stranger and deceiver whispering that she was never meant to be a mother, she encountered Norman, a man from her past. He lured her away with the promise of escaping all the pain, leading Delta to disappear without a word, leaving her children behind once more.

Upon Delta's disappearance, Louetta stepped in to care for her grand kids once again, continuing to pray with them and drop spiritual nuggets into their hearts every night. Months passed with no sign of Delta, and when she finally reappeared, Louetta had already made the decision to take the children to Georgia to visit Washington, inviting Delta to join them, but she refused. Detroit was like her Egypt, and she didn't want to leave. Not only that, but she was weighed down by the possibility of being pregnant with yet another child and was not sure if all the ones she had actually given birth to since her marriage were definitively Washington's.

As her kids ate in silence, she felt the weight of her choices, knowing she was about to lose them forever but unable to change her life, not able to fight for them over the yearning for the drug that called for her veins. It caused her to disappear and escape everything around her. To her, it was not a choice because she had no control over herself; she was in a prison and did not know how to escape. But she knew that she could choose to give her children something better by letting them go.

Jocelyn and Delmont, unaware of the internal struggle their mother carried, prepared to leave for Georgia, unsure when they would see her again. Jocelyn wiped away tears, already feeling the growing distance between them.

7

Sweet Georgia On My Mind

When Washington finally watched his children step out of the van onto Georgia soil, his heart soared. Jocelyn rushed into his arms, feeling safe and loved in a way she hadn't for so long. Delmont, however, kept his distance; his resentment toward his father was palpable. Washington knew he had to be patient, praying for the right moment to reconnect with his son.

As Washington embraced Jocelyn, he noticed his youngest child, Jamal, tumbling out of the van with an innocent curiosity. Barely old enough to grasp the weight of the situation, Jamal's wide eyes sparkled with wonder, unaware of the complexities surrounding their reunion. He giggled and took a few tentative steps on the unfamiliar ground, a reminder of the pure joy that could still exist amidst the tension. Washington smiled, feeling a renewed sense of hope

On Sunday, Washington took the children to church, where Jocelyn experienced something that would change her forever. Dressed in her Sunday best, she entered the sanctuary, over-whelmed by the Spirit of God and the unrestrained joy that filled the room. As the choir sang, she felt something stirring deep within her—an unfamiliar sensation, as if God was pursuing her through the music, whispering to her heart and singing over her with songs of deliverance (Zephaniah 3:17, NIV).

In that moment, Jocelyn clapped along with the congregation, tears of refreshment streaming down her cheeks. Surrounded by her father and grandmother, she felt an overwhelming sense of love and hope. God was pursuing Jocelyn, just as He had been all along, even in the darkest times—because even the darkness is light to Him (Psalm 139:12, TPT). The blueprint He placed inside of her containing His genetic code was communicating with her through the sounds of deliverance from the strokes of the keyboard (Genesis 1:27, TPT). Although she didn't fully understand this yet, every weapon forged by the enemy to inflict heartache would ultimately lead her to recognize the immeasurable strength she possessed (2 Corinthians 12:9-10, TPT), because what the enemy set out for harming her, God had already turned it around for her good, Jocelyn would learn that His goodness was impossible to escape.

In that moment, her pain said hello to hope, creating an indestructible force being built inside her. This was a sweet experience, a calling from the deep, a moment in time that she would never forget; this was how God pursued her.

Meanwhile, Jamal, Washington's youngest child, was nestled in his father's arms, blissfully unaware of the weighty conflicts surrounding him. At just a toddler, he clapped along to the music, his laughter a bright contrast to the heavier feelings in the room. Washington felt a swell of affection for Jamal, knowing that while he may not fully comprehend their family's struggles, his innocent joy was a welcome reminder of hope and new beginnings.

At first, their trip to Georgia was meant to be temporary.

Both Jocelyn and Delmont had promised Delta that they would return. They clung to that promise, hoping their absence might motivate Delta to get better. But as time passed, the peace and stability of Georgia began to feel like home. It seemed as if Washington had worked hard to create a safe space for them, something Delta had struggled to provide. This new reality presented Jocelyn and Delmont with conflicting emotions: they missed their mother, but their father's home was a refuge from the storm of their old life. This was the constructing of an understanding of the peace that Jocelyn would one day find on earth in her heavenly Father's dwelling place, the same shelter that her grandmother had been telling her about in Psalm 91.

Gradually, the idea of staying in Georgia became more of a possibility. Washington, seeing how well his children were adjusting, made plans for them to remain with him. He knew it was the best decision for their future, but he also understood the internal conflict they faced—keeping their promise to Delta or accepting the safety and love their father could provide.

In the end, the choice was made. Jocelyn and Delmont would stay with Washington in Georgia. However, even with this decision, Washington struggled with the thought of breaking Jamal's heart since he would have to send him back with his parents. At such a young age, Jamal was too little for Washington to care for as a single father. The road ahead was uncertain, but El Roi was watching, and Louetta had anchored her grandchildren with seeds of faith to keep them through any storm.

8

The Struggle for Identity

As the morning light filtered through the thin curtains of their modest Georgia home, Washington lay in bed, wrestling with his thoughts. His mind drifted to Delmont and Jocelyn, still tucked away in their beds. Being a single father wasn't something he had ever expected, and the weight of his responsibilities seemed heavier each day. Without Louetta around, Washington often felt lost. Louetta had been more than a mother—she had been his spiritual compass, the one who reminded him of what he was truly capable of. She planted seeds of faith that were meant to bloom and guide him, but Washington felt disconnected from those roots.

Despite Louetta's daily reminders, Washington struggled to fully embrace his true identity. The logical part of his mind often hindered his ability to accept the powerful truth of being a child of God, along with all the supernatural benefits that come with this acceptance (John 1:12, TPT). Rather than recognizing the divine invitation to become who God had always intended him to be, he misidentified himself based on the world around him, his past choices, and the circumstances those choices had created—such as broken relationships, financial struggles, and feelings of despair.

The challenge arises when we rely solely on perceptions shaped by the world; in doing so, we find ourselves walking in darkness (1 John 1:5, TPT). In that darkness, it becomes impossible to identify ourselves, because we have shut out the light, and without the light we cannot see our true reflection because the darkness intrudes to obscure our vision. This darkness was eroded by logic for Washington, causing him to be burdened by unnecessary weights, unaware that he could claim the victory that comes from being one of God's own (Romans 8:37, TPT).

All he needed to do was register himself with the "DMV of heaven" and receive his identification card, yet Washington didn't realize he was living a life that didn't belong to him—one that was misaligned with the divine DNA God had placed within him before he was born. He was meant to walk as a reflection of God's image and likeness, exercising divine authority and passing down that same generational blessing to his children. This lack of understanding put Jocelyn and Delmont at risk of inheriting a distorted perception of who they were created to be.

* * *

Every dollar Washington earned seemed to disappear, swallowed up by bills. On nights when the pressure became too much, he sought comfort at the bottom of a liquor bottle. This became his temporary escape, a refuge from the constant battlefield in his mind. But even in those dark moments, God was pursuing Washington—through unexpected blessings, like Mrs. Jenkins showing up with fresh vegetables or a side job landing in his lap right when he needed it. God was real, and Louetta knew it; she believed her prayers reached God concerning her child, no matter where he was located. So, she prayed for her son, that one day he would see it clearly and know how to identify with the God who was providing for him.

The word of God would sometimes whisper to Washington in his lowest moments: "The Lord is my shepherd; I lack nothing" (Psalm 23:1, TPT). While those words provided him with peace, since he wasn't actually living securely in the shelter of that peace, it wasn't enough to transform his mindset. The deeper issue was that Washington hadn't fully identified with Christ, and without that identification, he couldn't recognize his true inheritance—the inheritance of peace, joy, and dominion over all his worries. His internal struggles and undiagnosed depression clouded his understanding of God's plan for his life. These circumstances acted like a virus, creeping in to distort the intended information of his divine cellular structure, disrupting the preset design meant to guide him toward a full understanding and identification of who he was always meant to be. Instead, this virus sought to offer him a lie and perpetuated a contaminated false code of defeat and brokenness, confusing his mindset.

Jocelyn and Delmont had moved from one storm called Delta to another that settled in Washington, bringing with it clouds of unexpected fog. But somehow, even through the fog, Jocelyn was still able to see the sunlight. As she watched her father struggle in the storm of his emotions, she clung to the moments when God seemed to break through the chaos. She remembered the prayers her grandmother had taught them and how Lou-etta would pray over their home, inviting God's presence and protection as she declared Psalm 91. More than anything, she remembered how at the end of each prayer, Louetta would say, "In the Name of Jesus!" Jocelyn always felt settled by His name. Every time she heard "Jesus," something stirred inside her— something unexplainable from deep within, drawing her to an unknown place within herself. There was something about that name. Jocelyn was so grateful that her grandmother had taught her to call on the name of Jesus; she felt safety in that name, even if she didn't fully grasp who He was.

She would watch her father break down, heartache in one hand and alcohol in the other, wrestling with his pain. Despite witnessing his suffering, she held onto the belief that the God her grandmother spoke of had a plan for him. Even at a young age, Jocelyn understood that this was not the life her father was meant to lead. She was captivated by his intelligence; in her eyes, he could accomplish anything, even conquer the storm raging within him. She believed he had a purpose that extended beyond her and her brother, and she could see the greatness that lay within him. If only he could grasp that potential, she knew he could soar.

In those times, music became a means of connection between Jocelyn and her father. They often listened to songs by CeCe Winans, The Five Heartbeats, and Yolanda Adams—music that touched Jocelyn's soul. For the two of them, these songs were a temporary balm, soothing the deep pain that seemed to constantly bubble beneath the surface, like the eye of a storm waiting for the right agitation to come alive.

But when the music stopped and Jocelyn was no longer in the room, Washington was still left alone with his thoughts, one raging after the next, with no understanding of the true solution. Instead, he reflected his shattered identity deeper into the bottle and sometimes even into the arms of a woman, all serving as temporary fixes to put a band-aid over the deep, unspoken wounds he carried within himself.

Then, Washington started dating Carrie, who brought a motherly touch that Jocelyn desperately craved. Sadly, Carrie had her own wounds, coming from a family broken by addiction, racism, and rejection. But she loved Jocelyn and Delmont as if they were her own, and for the first time, Jocelyn felt the warmth of a mother's love. Carrie's presence in their lives was another act of God's pursuit, a reminder that He was always working things out for her good (Romans 8:28, TPT).

Still, the challenges remained. As Delmont grew, he struggled with his identity, drifting into the wrong crowd and joining a gang to find a place where he could belong. Jocelyn, looking up to her brother, began to imitate his behavior. However, when Delmont realized that hanging out with him put Jocelyn in danger, he forbade her from doing so. Understanding that he couldn't allow her to follow in his footsteps, he decided to confess everything to Washington in order to keep Jocelyn safe.

Now afraid for Jocelyn's life, Washington immediately set out to find a new home to protect his children from the trouble they were in, reaching out to his parents for help. Louetta, as always, responded with faith. She gathered the family together and prayed for a new home, asking God to make it a place of safety and blessing. And just like that, God provided.

For Jocelyn, these moments were more than just memories— they were the building blocks of her faith. She could feel God's presence in her life, pursuing her. She saw it in the way her grandmother's prayers were answered, in the music that touched her soul, and in the way God protected her, even when she didn't know she needed protecting.

As you continue to read Jocelyn's story, know that this is a story of how God pursues His own, relentlessly and lovingly, calling them back into His identity. God was in pursuit of Jocelyn, setting the stage to unveil her Christ identity. One day, Jocelyn would realize that all the trials and heartaches were not in vain. Even though suffering and harm were never her portion, God wouldn't waste it; instead, He would use the rubble to build an impenetrable palace, shaping every place within her and repairing her spaces with the fullness of His divine identity (Romans 8:16-17, TPT; John 3:6, TPT).

God had written His DNA into her very being (1 Peter 1:23, TPT), and no matter how dark things got, His light would always shine through (John 1:5, TPT). Jocelyn was destined for more, and if you are reading her story, you must grasp the truth that you are too—created in the image and likeness of God. Jocelyn's story is about Jesus and how He has marked the doorpost of our cellular structure with His divine DNA by paying the ransom to carry us into the family of His beloved children (1 Peter 1:18-19, TPT) and how we can recognize our identity as His children (Galatians 4:4-7, TPT; John 1:12, TPT).

9

The Pursuit Through Pain

After many years, Washington finally allowed Jocelyn and Delmont to visit their mother and the rest of their family in Detroit. When they arrived with Washington's sister, Joan, all of Delta's sisters were waiting for them. Their aunt Melanie was especially excited and promised the kids that she'd arrange for them to see their mother. Jocelyn and Delmont were filled with nervous anticipation, having been away from Delta for seven long years.

When Delta finally walked into Melanie's house, the moment hit Jocelyn like a punch in the gut. This woman didn't resemble the strong Black queen Jocelyn had idolized in her heart. Delta seemed empty—her eyes vacant, her posture detached. Jocelyn had held onto hope for all these years, refusing to believe Washington's words that their mother was a junkie who didn't want them. Now, standing before Delta, she felt a mix of excitement and dread.

Jocelyn, always the one with words, had written her mother a poem filled with hope and admiration. It described how she still saw Delta as a powerful figure, eager to offer inspiration and encouragement. But at that moment, Delta could not bear to look up at Jocelyn or the poem that passionately described Jocelyn's view of her mother. Tears welled up in her eyes as she fled from Jocelyn. Feigning a fit, Delta dropped the poem, walked out the door, and got into a car without even saying goodbye. The reality of their reunion felt more painful than Jocelyn had ever imagined.

For Jocelyn, this was the final fracture. She was devastated, her heart shattered in a way that felt beyond repair. This was a feeling of rejection that was too much to bear, and in that moment, Jocelyn decided that Delta would no longer have a place in her heart. She disowned her mother, vowing never to allow herself to feel this kind of pain again.

Back at her aunt's, the pain lingered, but Jocelyn found herself comforted by distractions. Her cousins and siblings took her and Delmont out to the streets of Detroit, where block parties, alcohol, and escape seemed to be the only way people knew how to cope with their problems. It didn't take long for Jocelyn to turn to alcohol, trying to drown her hurt. That night, as she downed drink after drink, she unknowingly walked further into the same generational cycle that had gripped both Delta and Washington. She stepped full force into the beast of addiction. Jocelyn was opening spiritual doors that gave the enemy access to wreak havoc on her life, without fully weighing the gravity of her actions and the consequences that could follow.

A few days later, Jocelyn and Delmont returned to Marietta just in time for Christmas. Shortly after their arrival, Louetta, their grandmother, came with their youngest brother, Jamal, bringing with her the warmth of love and the Spirit of God that always comforted Jocelyn. Aware of the struggles Jocelyn had faced with Delta, Louetta was determined to reach past the mess and connect with her granddaughter.

Louetta had a unique gift for touching the fragile places within her children and grandchildren, illuminating the darkness with her light. Jocelyn watched quietly, admiring the way her grandmother prayed every morning, engaging in heartfelt conversations with God, who was truly present with them. Though Jocelyn couldn't see Him, she sensed her grandmother's deep connection and longed to experience that same presence for herself.

One morning, Louetta asked Washington to play a CD for her. It was a powerful testimony by Helen Baylor. As Jocelyn sat at the edge of the stairs, listening to the gripping story of addiction and redemption, tears began to fall. Baylor spoke of her struggles with drugs, hitting rock bottom, and ultimately being saved by the prayers of her grandmother, who called on the name of Jesus.

As Jocelyn listened, she felt her heart stir. Every time she heard the name Jesus, it felt like a gentle tug—striking a spark of hope that He was more powerful than the pain and challenges she felt. There was something unexplainable about the name Jesus.

Louetta had been intentional about playing that testimony, hoping Jocelyn would hear it. She wanted her granddaughter to understand that no one, not even Delta, was beyond the reach of Jesus. In that moment, Jocelyn began to hope again. Jocelyn's wounds were still raw from her encounter with Delta, but in the depths of her pain, God was sowing seeds in her that would one day grow into a deeper understanding of His love—a love so amazing that it could transcend time and repair even the years of what was lost or wasted. This is how God was pursuing her even through her pain.

However, Jocelyn still hadn't surrendered, and the rebellion only intensified. After Delmont was taken from her and sent to juvenile detention due to his involvement in gang activity, Jocelyn's behavior spiraled out of control. Drinking became her primary coping mechanism, and she frequently snuck out, sinking deeper into trouble.

One night, she ran away and stayed with a friend's family in Forest Park. It was there that a terrifying incident occurred— one that left Jocelyn feeling even more lost and confused. After drinking heavily, she woke up next to an unfamiliar man, at least ten years older than her, with no memory of what had happened. The fragments she recalled suggested she may have been drugged, leaving her scarred, confused, and struggling to cope with the trauma.

After this tragic event, Jocelyn was ready to find her way back home to her father, and Washington was overjoyed that his daughter had returned. But when she came back, he could see the pain in her eyes. He knew something had shifted in his daughter in a deeply unsettling way. It was the same look he had seen in Delta—the look of someone who had buried an unspeakable sorrow deep within their soul.

Washington didn't press her for answers. He wasn't sure how to comfort her, but he knew God could. So, he prayed that God would heal his daughter, even as he struggled to hold himself together.

Still struggling to cope with the horror she faced in Forest Park, Jocelyn's rebellion deepened. She began skipping school, drinking heavily, dating older boys, and running away from home more frequently. Washington, at a loss for how to help her—and fighting to control his own temper in the face of her behavior—decided to send her to live with his sister, Joan. He hoped that a change of environment, surrounded by family and the church, might pull Jocelyn back from the edge.

As he watched her leave, Washington whispered a desperate prayer: "Lord, please save my baby. Don't let her be like me or her mother."

What Washington couldn't see was that God was already at work, pursuing Jocelyn in ways that were beyond his understanding. The divine DNA that had been planted in her was still there, untarnished by the pain and rebellion, just waiting for the right moment in time to activate His genetic code within her (1 Peter 1:23, TPT; Ecclesiastes 3:1, TPT). God's original blueprint for her life was unshakable (Jeremiah 1:5, TPT; Romans 8:29, TPT), and He was calling her through the darkness into His marvelous light. Jocelyn's story wasn't over—God was the author of her life, pursuing her with relentless love (Galatians 4:4-5, TPT; Ephesians 1:11, TPT).

10

The Call

After years of living with the weight of her broken experiences, Jocelyn sat on the edge of her seat in this little white church around the corner from her aunt's house, her heart racing as she listened intently to the preacher speak about Jesus—this man Who was a man but also God. He was God in a body of flesh, and He healed the sick, cast out demons, and transformed lives. The words flowed like a river of hope, washing over her as he described how He tore darkness apart with light and overtook everything around Him with His glory.

With each fervent word, hope surged within her, mingling with racing questions that felt almost too fragile to voice. Could this Jesus heal her mother too, the woman who had always battled the chains of addiction, whose life had been a constant struggle against her demons? Could He fix the broken pieces of her life, the ones that felt irreparably shattered? She longed to believe it with every fiber of her being.

As the preacher spoke of Jesus enduring betrayal and suffering so that others could live in freedom, something re-calibrated within Jocelyn. Warmth spread through her chest, and she finally began to understand why this name held such power. It wasn't just a name; it was a person, and He was real, alive, and available—and He wanted her. The thought of Him was overwhelming, exhilarating, and irresistible all at once.

Tears began to well up in her eyes, shimmering like fragile glass, and she felt her pain lift, as though Jesus Himself was taking it from her with every lash that He endured. The weight of her sorrow was being absorbed by the very One who had suffered for her freedom. It was a release, a letting go that she hadn't known she needed.

In that unforgettable moment, surrounded by the soft glow of faith and the warmth of community, Jocelyn closed her eyes, allowing the tears to flow freely. In each tear, it was like a small glimpse of who she was meant to be was reflected in every word about Jesus that the preacher spoke. She could see a flicker of someone that resembled her but wasn't her, trying to break through. As each tear dropped, it sprung up hope for what could be—a hope that whispered of redemption not just for Jocelyn but for her mother too.

The walls around her heart began to fall. Years of cemented pain, abandonment, and rejection began to crack under the weight of Jesus' relentless love. As the psalmist began to sing, "Silver and Gold, I'd rather have Jesus than silver and gold," Jocelyn's heart was overcome. She thought deep inside, "I'd rather have You too, Jesus!" She knew Jesus was calling her, and she couldn't resist. Every word of the song gripped her soul. When the psalmist sang, "I called on Jesus, my life He can hold," Jocelyn lost control, overwhelmed by the love of God. She felt God's pursuit of her, and she was ready to surrender to His relentless love. Her life had been hard and heartbreaking, but her life He could hold, and He had been holding it this whole time.

Without even realizing how she had walked and made it to the altar, she was there before the church confessing Jesus as her Lord and Savior. It was like an out-of-body experience; she felt like she had been rescued, snatched from the jaws of darkness and translated into a kingdom of love. It was more real than anything she'd ever known.

Weeks later, Jocelyn lay in bed, lost in thoughts of her mother and father. A deep sadness enveloped her as she watched her cousins laughing and embraced by both their parents. She longed for that connection, that sense of wholeness, and felt a deep emptiness in her heart. Surrounded by family yet feeling utterly alone, she wept quietly, her tears soaking the pillow beneath her.

As she lay there, overwhelmed by her grief, she suddenly felt a presence beside her—a warmth that wrapped around her like a comforting blanket. It was as if someone had entered her room and settled in beside her. In that stillness, a tender voice echoed within her and all around her, whispering gently, "When your father and mother abandon you, I will make you mine" (Psalm 27:10, TPT).

In that moment, something shifted. Every thought of abandonment and loneliness began to melt away. Jocelyn felt the weight of her sorrow lift, replaced by a deep sense of safety and love. She closed her eyes and surrendered to the embrace of what she knew to be her Heavenly Father. No longer isolated in her pain, she felt His arms around her, strong and unwavering, assuring her that she was never truly alone.

Tears flowed freely, but this time they were not just tears of sorrow; they were tears of release, of recognition that she was cherished and wanted. In the depths of her heart, she understood that even amidst her struggles, she belonged to Him. And for the first time in what felt like an eternity, Jocelyn felt a glare of hope—a whisper of a promise that she was loved beyond measure.

From that day, her desires began to change. She no longer craved the things that once held her captive. Cigarettes, alcohol, and rebellion began to lose their grip. Under the guidance of her aunt Joan, Jocelyn found strength in prayer; talking to Jesus became a place of dwelling and safety. Joan recognized the potential in her niece and encouraged her to tap into her gift of writing; she was always pouring life-giving words into Jocelyn's heart.

But she had not yet embraced her new identity that had been trying to show itself through her tears in that little white church. She accepted the freedom and relief that salvation brought, but she didn't recognize the full scope of this salvation—she did not know that she had been rescued from a fallen identity (Genesis 1). The identity that said she was like her mother and her father, whom she dearly loved, but this identity in them was one of earthly things, of natural things, of the flesh, and of all of the broken places she had found within herself. So while she was saved, and her identity that was stolen before the fall had been restored, she had not yet seen herself unfolded in Jesus (2 Corinthians 5:17, TPT). Even though her real identity had returned the minute she received Christ's invitation, she had not yet accepted this recovered identity.

She was still carrying the weight of other people's perceptions about who she was, stuck in the shadow of "Black Delta." Everyone constantly said she was a copy of her mother—same looks, same attitude, same future. And for a long time, Jocelyn saw her identity in that perception. She thought her mother's toughness and beauty were something to admire. Even though Delta was an addict, there was still something about her that made Jocelyn want to be just like her. What little girl doesn't find something about her mother to look up to?

But the hard truth was this: being like Delta meant inheriting not only her boldness but also her struggles. Delta's sharp tongue and fierce independence often masked the turmoil beneath the surface. To emulate her meant grappling with intense pain, using words as shields, and navigating the complexities of relationships with caution, always leaving walls up to keep pain from creeping through. It involved confronting addiction and making choices that could lead to heartache; it meant being detached even from your children, all while searching for the love and nurturing that felt just out of reach.

Delta may have commanded effortless respect on the streets; even as a drug addict, people seemed to be swept away with her, but deep within, she wrestled with her own battles. Jocelyn didn't fully grasp that following in her mother's footsteps could lead her down a dangerous path that mirrored Delta's pain.

She wasn't meant to live in Delta's shadow; she had been created for something far greater. She had been given a new identity, restored as a daughter of God, with the promise of freedom, purpose, and wholeness. However, because Jocelyn didn't fully understand this truth, she remained trapped in the belief that salvation was merely about escaping hell and alleviating her pain.

Living like that is like a butterfly that thinks it's still a caterpillar, never realizing the wings it's been given. Jocelyn had the power to fly, but without embracing her true identity, she stayed grounded—trapped in the very cycle she was meant to break free from.

Returning to her father's house eventually after the school year was over, Washington was still battling his demons—his mental illness and alcoholism had worsened, and he was unable to offer Jocelyn the spiritual guidance she needed. He went to church but not as consistently as her aunt.

Matthew 12:43-45 warns that a house that has been swept clean but left empty is vulnerable to spirits returning, stronger than before. That's exactly what happened to Jocelyn.

Without community, prayer, a spiritual covering, or under-standing of what she needed at only the age of 14, Jocelyn found herself falling back into old patterns. When she turned 16, J.R. entered her life. He appeared to be the love she had been longing for, someone who seemed to care about her and offer her the attention and affection she craved. Before long, Jocelyn was pregnant with his child, and Washington was heartbroken; he felt her whole future was down the drain. It wasn't long after the news of the pregnancy that her newfound love quickly spiraled into something dark. J.R. began to abuse her, physically and emotionally. The more J.R. hurt her, the more she clung to him, not realizing that she was repeating the cycle of brokenness; she was becoming Black Delta.

The abuse started months after Jocelyn found out she was pregnant, and months after the abuse, she gave birth to Zion. She tried to be the mother she had always longed to have, but the weight of abuse, addiction, and the unresolved trauma from her past kept flooding back in like a tsunami, wreaking havoc on her. She was walking in the same patterns that had caused Delta to lose her children. Every time J.R. hit her, and every time she reached for the bottle to numb the pain, she unknowingly opened doors and aligned herself with the broken identity that had been placed on her when she passed through the womb (Psalm 51:5, TPT)—Delta's and Washington's brokenness, which became the mirror through which she saw herself.

As the abuse escalated, Jocelyn spiraled deeper. J.R.'s beatings became more frequent, more violent, and each time, she found herself reaching for worse and worse forms of escape until DFACS came and took Zion, leaving her alone to reflect on how she had become the resemblance of Black Delta.

That's when Wallace entered her life. He was Washington's sister Joan's nephew, someone who had grown up around her family, and in many ways, Wallace seemed like a rescuer. He stepped in when J.R.'s abuse had gotten out of hand, pulling Jocelyn out of a toxic situation and offering her a way out.

Wallace seemed to be everything she needed at the time—stable, familiar, and willing to fight for her. But soon enough, Wallace's rescue turned into a nightmare. Wallace became abusive too, and his abuse was worse than J.R.'s. While J.R. had been physically abusive, Wallace was mentally, emotionally, and physically abusive, controlling Jocelyn in every way possible. He told her how to dress, wouldn't allow her to talk to other men, dictated when she could go outside, how many hours a day she could work, and constantly berated her with insults. His affairs with other women were frequent, and he made sure she knew he was in control.

Wallace moved her away from her family, which at first seemed like a good thing—a fresh start—but it was a calculated move to isolate her. She was cut off from her support system, left to deal with his increasing abuse on her own. With every level of abuse, Jocelyn found herself diving deeper into addiction. As the last ounce of control she had over herself, Wallace introduced her to cocaine, and it quickly became her escape from the torment she was living through. As her drug use escalated, she teetered on the verge of something worse. The more isolated and addicted she became, the further she spiraled.

Jocelyn eventually had a child with Wallace, a son. But even having a second child didn't stop the downward spiral. Wallace's abuse continued, and Jocelyn's dependence on cocaine grew. Her identity had become more fragmented than it had ever been, shattered by layers of abuse, addiction, and brokenness. She had started out believing Wallace was her rescuer, but now she was trapped again, this time in a deeper pit than ever before. Besides, no one could have ever been her rescuer but God, and He was calling her out by her name, trying to get her to see to come back to Him (Isaiah 44:21-22, TPT).

Jocelyn was losing control; the more she used drugs to escape, the more her life unraveled. She had already lost custody of Zion. Now, she found herself in the same position as her mother— losing her child to the father's family, just like Delta had lost her children to their father's family years before. But God's pursuit of her never stopped. Even as she lost Zion, even as she fell deeper into addiction, God was still whispering to her heart, reminding her of the truth of her identity. The world, her circumstances, and the enemy had all tried to rewrite her story, to make her believe that she was destined to repeat Delta's fate. But God had placed His DNA inside of her from the very beginning. He had written her story long before the trauma and brokenness entered.

Though she had lost her son and fallen into this cycle of abuse and addiction, God was not done with her. The enemy had used her circumstances to try to distort her identity, to make her identify with where she had come from in the natural, trying to hide the fact that she had been born from another realm. She only needed to see herself from her Father's view—from God's view. He was still pursuing her, reminding her that she was more than the sum of the choices she had made, more than the abuse she had endured. She was His own prized possession, carrying His divine DNA, and the battle for her soul was one God had already won. She only needed to sit down and let Jesus take His rightful place of rule in her life.

She was not ready to take her seat, so she stood at the edge of complete destruction. She was not tuned in to the frequency of God's voice that was calling out to her. He was louder than the lies—she just needed to be still to hear Him. If she could only understand that He was a strong tower, stronger than any pain she had endured. He had endured so much more for her. Jocelyn was not Delta or Washington. She was God's, created in His image, with His purpose and plan embedded in her very being. And no amount of pain, rebellion, or addiction could change that truth. As she spiraled, even as she made her bed in the lowest places, He was there (Psalm 139:8, TPT; Isaiah 43:1, TPT).

11

The Call to True Identity

Jocelyn's downward spiral wasn't just a fall into drugs and promiscuity—it was the complete obscuring of her identity, a version of herself that had been hidden, lost, and shattered. Much like traffickers erase the identities of their victims, branding them with who they think they should be, Jocelyn had been tricked by the lies of the enemy that sought to label her by her circumstances and mold her by the broken world that surrounded her (John 10:10, TPT). The true version of who she was meant to be—the one created in God's image—was buried beneath layers of deception and pain. Yet, even in her deepest pain and rebellion, God was relentlessly pursuing her, refusing to let the enemy's brand define her. Just as traffickers try to claim ownership of their victims, the enemy had tried to claim her. But she belonged to God, and He goes after His own. He was set on reclaiming what belonged to Him, refusing to allow anything to separate her from Him, even in the darkest moments as she tried to run from the shame of all she felt she had become (Romans 8:38-39, TPT). God was right there, calling her back to her true identity as His own (Isaiah 43:1, TPT).

Finally, Jocelyn left Wallace and moved back in with her father, Washington, where her cousins were also staying. This environment of old wounds and unresolved issues bred even more recklessness. Freed from Wallace's control and what, at the time, felt like the heavy responsibility of motherhood, Jocelyn threw herself into a life of drugs, alcohol, and promiscuity. Each moment was spent high, chasing fleeting pleasures, and doing whatever it took to make money—including selling anything and anyone. Everything and everyone had a price tag to Jocelyn, and she leveraged it all. It got to the point where she felt unrecognizable, as though the world, her family, and even she no longer knew who she truly was. She was no longer identifiable even as Black Delta, but something and someone far worse, yet at the same time, somehow identified by everything she was doing.

She fell so low that she even managed to get entangled in all kinds of legal issues and, little by little, began racking up a criminal record. One of the lowest points came one night when, in a drunken rage, she nearly killed her cousin during a heated fight. She sank even lower when, riding in the back seat to a party one night, she decided to jump out of the car on the highway in the middle of steady traffic. It was only by the grace of God that Jocelyn was still alive. She had really started to believe that she was too damaged, beyond redemption, and that her identity was forever shattered.

But what she didn't know was that Jesus had already spoken: He finishes what He starts (Philippians 1:6, TPT), and if He began a work, He brings it to completion. She just needed to grab hold of this truth! The truth was that she was already complete in Christ (Colossians 2:10, TPT), and until she truly grasped hold of it, her life would keep spinning out of control.

This spiral took her back to Detroit, where she stayed with her sister, hoping to reconnect with her mother, Delta. But Detroit, with its easy access to drugs, only buried her deeper in her addiction. On the upside, after years of distance, Jocelyn finally saw her mother again. She was so excited for this day until she came face to face with Delta. Her mother was enveloped by drugs, living in a filthy, abandoned house, and unable to even recognize her own daughter. Jocelyn's heart broke into pieces—pieces that only the Potter could ever put back together (Jeremiah 18:6, TPT). Delta's blank, unseeing eyes and the needle hanging from her arm were a mirror for Jocelyn—a reflection of where her own life was headed if nothing changed. Deep down, Jocelyn knew she was walking the same destructive path. She knew in that moment a change had to happen, but she couldn't see her way out. She was in the wilderness and needed a stream (Isaiah 43:18-19, TPT).

Haunted by the encounter with her mother, Jocelyn returned to Georgia. Her stepmother, Carrie, had moved into a house directly across from a little white church. Jocelyn moved in with Carrie, but she was still playing around in her destructive behavior. However, God's pursuit of her was becoming undeniable. This church, only ten steps away, blared worship music twice a week that Jocelyn could hear every time she stepped outside. The pastor would come outside while she was high as a kite, look her right in the eyes with love, and call her by name, inviting her to come inside. Jocelyn didn't understand at the time, but it was God Himself calling her by name, not the pastor (Isaiah 43:1, TPT). Just like when God called Hagar in her wilderness of despair (Genesis 16:7-8, TPT), He was calling Jocelyn's name through this pastor. He was wooing her into His loving arms through the music, which seemed to intensify the beat of her heart with every string and note that was sung (Romans 5:8, TPT).

Yet, Jocelyn, too caught up in her pain and shame to believe she could be redeemed, resisted the Lover of her soul a little longer. She didn't understand that she was wanted by God, even in her brokenness (Romans 5:8, TPT). He was daring her to come home so that He could put back together all the shattered pieces and give her back her stolen identity (Luke 15:20, TPT).

Hollowing in her rebellion, she hit another devastating breaking point when she lost custody of her second son, Edward. Drunk and reckless, she put him in harm's way, and the police intervened. Watching them take him away felt like the last piece of her heart was being ripped out. Jocelyn blamed everyone— Edward's father, the police, even God—but couldn't face the truth that her own choices had led her to this point. Unable to confront her responsibility, she numbed herself with more drugs, more alcohol, and more reckless choices.

Drifting from one couch to another, Jocelyn burned bridges with every friend she had left. She destroyed relationships with every family member, some beyond repair. She even burned her last bridge with Carrie. She sank deeper into bitterness and grief, mourning the mother she had lost, the children she had failed, and the future she had once dreamed of. She believed the lie that she was never meant to be a mother, just as her own mother had failed her. Jocelyn convinced herself that God had made a mistake in allowing her to have children, and she resigned herself to a life of self-destruction, living in complete duress.

Jocelyn sat on the edge of the bed, her heart heavy with the weight of her choices. As she looked around the dim room, a vision started to form in her mind—a glimpse of an older version of herself, confident and full of life, yet feeling so far out of reach.

She also saw the life she could keep living, one filled with the promise of wealth but also the pain of destruction. The struggle within her was intense, and she felt God pulling at her heart.

In that moment, everything became clear as God's light illuminated her darkness, giving her the chance to choose a different path. Sitting next to her last remaining friend, Charisma, Jocelyn broke down. "Are you tired?" she asked, her voice shaking with emotion. Tears streamed down her face as she realized how exhausted she was—tired of running from God, tired of the lies, and worn out by the brokenness surrounding her.

Feeling a sense of urgency, she grabbed her phone and called her father, Washington. "Can you take me to the little white church across from Carrie's house?" she said, understanding that every time that preacher had called her name, it was really God calling out to her, inviting her out of the darkness and into His light, and she was ready to surrender.

Like Jonah, who found himself in the belly of the fish (Jonah 1:17), Jocelyn had tried to escape God's command of her heart but now felt trapped by God's unwavering love. In that moment of vulnerability, she knew that surrender was the only way forward. She thought of Washington, her earthly father, who, despite his flaws and struggles, had always been there for her. He never stopped reaching out, asking her to come back home. His love reflected the constant, faithful love of God.

That Sunday morning, despite having been out partying all night, Jocelyn walked into that little white church fully ready to receive every instruction God had for her. The pastor was preaching on the story of Abraham, and the message immediately struck a deep chord within her. He spoke about how God had called Abraham out of Haran—a place of pain, loss, and stagnation—and into a land of promise. Haran symbolized the place where Abraham's journey was stuck, where he had lost his brother and stayed too long, but God was calling him to leave everything familiar and step into the unknown where His promises awaited.

For Jocelyn, Marietta was her Haran. It was the place where her identity had been stained and muddied—where she had come to know the abandonment of family and friends, and where she had been abused; a place where she became confused, where she was stuck after losing her mother and both of her children. It was the place where she began her downward spiral into addiction and destruction; it was the place where the scariest version of herself tried to take its place, and it was the place that that version of herself would be dethroned. Like Abraham, she had stayed long enough in a place that symbolized loss, trauma, brokenness, and, more than anything, weakness. As the pastor spoke, it was as if God was speaking directly to Jocelyn's heart, calling her out of her Haran, out of her pain and her past, and into something new. But she would have to be willing to leave behind everything she knew, even the familiar pain that she had become all too comfortable with, to step into the future God had for her.

This message unraveled her because she awakened to the fact that God had been pursuing her all along, to rewrite all the contaminated information that had entered her soul about who she was and whose she was. In that moment, Jocelyn found the courage she had been lacking. God was calling her to leave her Haran, and she had the strength to obey, but it wasn't her strength; it was something supernatural.

A few weeks later, Jocelyn checked herself into rehab. It wasn't just a decision to get sober; it was a full surrender to God's will for her life. It was during rehab that Jocelyn finally faced the truth she had been running from. As the fog of addiction cleared, she began to confront the deep wounds she had been carrying—her abandonment of her children, her betrayal of loved ones, and the guilt of her destructive patterns. The hardest part of her recovery wasn't forgiving others; it was forgiving herself.

In rehab, Jocelyn's healing wasn't just physical—it was spiritual. The rehab facility had a church that offered transportation to anyone willing to attend, and Jocelyn found herself on that van every Sunday. Slowly, as she journaled her prayers and read her Bible, she started to come back to herself and back to her God, secured and safe in Him. She prayed fervently for her mother's deliverance, believing that if God could restore her, He could restore Delta too. God's grace had rewritten Jocelyn's story, and now she was ready to fully step into the life He had planned for her (Jeremiah 29:11, TPT).

After fourteen months in rehab, Jocelyn was ready to step back into the world. Her life had been restored in ways she never imagined. She reconnected with her sons, Edward and Zion. But the greatest sign of restoration came when she received a phone call—her mother, Delta, had been sober for ten months; that's how long Jocelyn had been in rehab minus two months! After 26 years of addiction, God had worked a miracle in Delta's life, just as He had done for Jocelyn

12

Known by God

Jocelyn's journey to rediscovering herself in Christ was nothing short of miraculous. The woman who had once spiraled into addiction, drug enterprising, and a life of promiscuity under a complete identity crisis had now been transformed into someone new! Her life had undergone a complete reconstruction— she had been entirely remodeled. And it all began with a single "yes" to God in that little white church—a decision that changed the course of her life forever.

After graduating from rehab, Jocelyn reconnected with her mother. For the next six years, they built a loving and cherished relationship until Delta passed away. While Jocelyn still had areas of growth and some parts of her life were still under construction, she often saw herself reflected in Delta's influence. For the longest time, she had believed she had no choice but to mirror her mother's life, thinking her nature was predetermined by Delta's past.

During this time of self-discovery, God brought Richmond into Jocelyn's life. When she met Richmond, they instantly fell in love. She couldn't believe it—he was everything she had asked God for on that piece of paper she had hidden away in her Bible. He was kind, respectful, and different from anyone she had ever known, treating her like royalty—something she had never experienced from a man.

Richmond was like her prince charming, dismantling every wall she had built around herself to avoid being hurt again. His persistent pursuit was exactly what Jocelyn desperately needed. With Richmond, she felt no need to hold up barriers; his love and care allowed her to open her heart fully. He was truly a Godsend, and his unwavering affection constantly reminded her of how deeply she was loved and valued—not only by him but also by God. Within a year, their love had blossomed so much that they decided to make it official and marry.

Jocelyn felt this same overwhelming joy when she gave birth to their daughter, Charity. Charity was a testament to God's love for her. She was everything Jocelyn had prayed for, right down to the very color of her skin. It amazed her that the God who created the universe—the One who called light into darkness (Genesis 1:3, TPT), formed the earth, set captives free, orchestrated miracles, and parted seas—had heard her voice. She had delighted in Him, and He had taken note of her desires and brought them to life (Psalm 37:4, TPT). This realization strengthened her faith, drawing her into deeper trust and affection for God as she found refuge under His shadow. She realized that Psalm 91 had been watching over her entire life, pursuing her through every twist and turn.

Moments like these reminded Jocelyn of how God's love had always been in pursuit of her. He had wooed her, protected her, and loved her through every pitfall. And He didn't just save her to walk this earth broken and shattered; that was merely the residue of the dead woman buried with Jesus! Her past had been nailed to the cross, sealing the tomb where the old Jocelyn—the one who passed through her mother's birth womb—was laid to rest.

Knowing she was known by God, saved, and called by name was powerful, but it wasn't the full picture. Salvation, as wonderful and secure as it is, was only one part of what God had done. Yes, she had been saved by grace (Ephesians 2:8, TPT), but she still felt incomplete. She struggled with viewing herself merely as a sinner saved by grace, relying on God yet never fully stepping into the identity that had been secured for her in Jesus Christ (Colossians 3:3, TPT). He had called her out of darkness and into His love—but for what purpose, and to what destiny?

13

Returned Identification

Jocelyn's transformation was remarkable, and God strategically used her children to help her find a church home. Aware of her past mistakes, she understood the importance of connecting with a community of believers. All she really wanted was to immerse herself in the Word; she envisioned sitting at the feet of Jesus, soaking up every word He spoke (Luke 10:39, TPT). The more she surrendered to God, the more He broke destructive behaviors from her life—behaviors she hadn't even realized existed.

Though the church was small, it provided a safe community where Jocelyn formed healthy connections. She began to see herself differently and value herself beyond what the world had told her (1 Peter 2:9, TPT). Jocelyn loved attending church; it became her top priority. When her church was closed, she would visit another one. If she could have, she would have slept in a church.

She discovered a women's ministry within walking distance from her home and began attending regularly, forming a close friendship with the woman who ran it. This ministry became a space where Jocelyn felt comfortable speaking up and testifying about God's presence and all He had done in her life (Revelation 12:11, TPT). Each time she testified, the shame of her past faded further.

Catherine, the woman who led the ministry, reignited Jocelyn's love for poetry. Catherine organized talent nights where women could showcase the gifts God had given them (1 Peter 4:10, TPT). Encouraged by Catherine, Jocelyn wrote her first poem in years. Although she initially wanted to keep it to herself, she found laughter, fellowship, and connection with these women. She was able to open up, be free, and share what God had placed inside of her. Writing was something that was close to therapy for Jocelyn, but it was a blessing for her to find out that these words also had the power to soothe someone else's heart.

At times, Jocelyn found herself in awe of how much her life had changed. She remembered when fun meant walking through downtown Atlanta high and drunk, surrounded by friends who were strippers, escorts, or drug dealers. Now, her friends were ministers, pastors, and prophets (2 Corinthians 5:17, TPT). Her life had taken a complete 360, and sometimes she could barely recognize the girl she used to be. Old things had certainly passed away, and all things had truly become new.

When God does reconstruction, He changes everything from the inside out. He not only reconstructed Jocelyn but also reconstructed her environment so that nothing could creep back in to disrupt His divine structure (Romans 12:2, TPT). God placed many powerhouse women in her life to help develop, love, and nurture her. Jocelyn had found true sisters in Christ (Galatians 6:2, TPT).

Jocelyn became aware that with every word she spoke, she took more power from the principalities and forces of darkness, making a stand that she would be and do what God said (Jeremiah 1:9, TPT). She made up her mind to be an example of how God can take what the world may have viewed as nothing and make something to become a display of His glory (1 Corinthians 1:27, TPT). The only problem was that Jocelyn's desire was to shine through her writing and serve in the background—hiding in the shadows and helping wherever she could. But the more she tried to hide, the more God pulled her out of the shadows. It wasn't just her poetry; God wanted to use her testimony. All of her broken places seemed to have the power to bring someone else out of theirs because of the reconciling power of Jesus Christ. He used His testimony of deliverance in Jocelyn's life to draw people out of the darkest places (Matthew 5:16, TPT). After all, if Jesus did it for her, He could do it for anybody. In fact, He had already done it for everybody; they only had to accept.

* * *

Then one day at a church service, Jocelyn met a woman who changed her life. There is a path for every person's life, a path of defining. This was Jocelyn's day. Sitting shyly by herself, she was taken by surprise when the woman approached her and said, "Hi, I just wanted to tell you that you have such a light and presence of God surrounding you." Confused, Jocelyn looked around, wondering if she was speaking to her. But as she turned to face this woman, she felt an instant connection. She wondered who she was and, even more, why she approached her. Jocelyn felt an instant connection; it was instantly deep for her.

Up until this day, Jocelyn had been delivered from her bondage, but she had not been truly free. She didn't know who she was, and just like her mother had unintentionally defined Jocelyn from the womb, it took another mother to undo it—to give her a new definition, to dismantle every lie and label that had ever been placed on Jocelyn. This was her mother, her spiritual mother, someone that God had sent to reach down into the darkest places inside of Jocelyn and draw out the light that was always within her—the light that would illuminate the information that was written on her DNA structure. A mother looks at her children and sees right past everything else, looking into who she knows her child is. A mother doesn't let anything else define her children because she resigns that right; that is why a mother names a child at their birth. Sometimes, God will send a spiritual mother or father to redefine His children when they have been misidentified and defined incorrectly. When Jocelyn met Zoe, that is what happened.

This woman refused to acknowledge any brokenness in Jocelyn; she saw beyond. All she would acknowledge was the wholeness that Jesus had already completed in her. God had sent her to open Jocelyn's eyes and return her to her true identity, the one hidden in Christ (Ephesians 1:18, TPT). She demanded that Jocelyn begin to see herself the same way—that she shed all the limitations of her biological nature that told her she had to identify with anything in a fallen state. She urged her to understand herself as being born again from spirit and from water, born again from the Spirit of God. As a child of God, His nature was her only union. She labored to open Jocelyn's eyes to the truth that she had always been as God had always intended—created in the image and likeness of God. She nurtured Jocelyn into this truth, that through Jesus, she had been reconciled back to the original intent, the person planned in Christ Jesus before the foundation of the world.

In these moments, as God used Zoe's voice as the womb in which the Spirit and water began to remold her, Jocelyn was being carried in a spiritual womb, imparted with a lineage that would forever change the course of her life. She stepped into a new awareness of herself, realizing that her identity was not defined by her past, her biology, her mistakes, or her pain, but by who God had always said she was: His own possession, His beloved, the apple of His eye (1 Peter 2:9, TPT). Zoe demanded that Jocelyn accept this truth—she was no longer broken. In Christ Jesus, broken things do not exist. In fact, the moment she stepped into Christ, believing that He had traded places with every corrupt thing concerning her, she embraced her completion. As His daughter, she carried within her the incorruptible seed of God—a royal DNA that set her apart (1 Peter 1:23, TPT). Finally, she was ready to accept her Kingdom Identification card and all the benefits it granted her access to (Philippians 3:20, TPT). She was now able to step out of the definitions of every label she had been marked with in this world and receive the seal of God's kingdom.

Jocelyn's story is proof that God's possessions are not actually broken; the world around them is broken, causing them to be misidentified. But His relentless pursuit draws the one who is willing back to who He has defined them to be. He goes after His own by whatever means necessary (Luke 19:10, TPT). If He has called you, make no mistake—He will not lose you (John 10:27-29, TPT). Jocelyn began to grasp that she was not just saved but empowered (Acts 1:8, TPT). She reached a point where she refused to live beneath her identity in Jesus and rejected any limitations the world tried to impose on her. Despite her criminal background, she pursued a career in criminal justice. Throughout college, the enemy attempted to convince her that she would never prosper because of her past, but she put him beneath her feet, where he belonged, and pursued her degree (Romans 16:20, TPT). Later, she became a probation officer, eager to empower others in their own journeys of redemption and rehabilitation (2 Corinthians 1:3-4, TPT).

Jesus' declaration, "It is finished" (John 19:30, TPT), was not just about her salvation; it signified the completion of everything: sickness, brokenness, poverty, dysfunction, and death (Isaiah 53:4-5, TPT). The moment she accepted Jesus at 14, her old self passed away, and she was given the authority to be God's image-bearer on earth (2 Corinthians 5:17; Genesis 1:27, TPT). While she may not have been ready to fully embrace her identity at 14, she had now arrived at a place of impact and embrace. She had met someone who revealed to her what she truly held inside (Colossians 3:3, TPT).

The Spirit of the Supreme God of the Universe had taken up residence in her—the One through whom all things exist (Colossians 1:16, TPT). She was a co-heir with Him (Romans 8:17, TPT). Just as DNA contains the information that determines a person's appearance, thoughts, and actions, it reveals their character, nature, and abilities (Psalm 139:14, TPT). We find our true DNA in the Word of God, who is Jesus, serving as our instruction manual (2 Timothy 3:16-17, TPT). The Word of God is a seed, and seeds carry DNA that shapes who we are (Luke 8:11, TPT). When we immerse ourselves in Christ, who is the Word (John 1:1, TPT), we behold what we are meant to become, embodying the nature and character of our Abba, Daddy (Romans 8:15, TPT).

With this understanding of her identity, the labels the world and her environment had placed on her—criminal, addict, failure, "just like Delta"—were revealed as lies (John 8:32, TPT). There was now a demand on Jocelyn's life to walk in the truth that everything in her past had passed away (2 Corinthians 5:17, TPT). The defeated woman she once was had died, and in her place stood a new creation—a creation in Christ (Galatians 2:20, TPT). When you decide to step into Christ, you are restored to His image, no longer defined by your past (Ephesians 4:24, TPT). Christ is impenetrable and unstoppable, and if He lives in you, then so are you (1 John 4:4, TPT).

If you have already accepted your identity and found yourself in Christ Jesus, live today with unshakable faith in the knowledge of who you are. You are a son or daughter of God the Most High, victorious in Christ (1 John 5:4, TPT). I ignite you to walk in the fullness of God's divine purpose for your life (Romans 8:37, TPT). And if you are not in Christ Jesus, take hold of this invitation to receive Him as your Lord (Romans 10:9-10, TPT).

Accept your true identification in Christ Jesus!

Afterword

As I reached the completion of this book, I found myself reflecting on the myriad experiences and influences that brought it to life. Writing has been both a challenge and a privilege, allowing me to explore my thoughts and feelings in a way that I hope resonates with you.

This work is a tapestry woven from the threads of my relationships, experiences, and faith. Each thought shared is a glimpse into my life, shaped by love and endurance, the strength of my friends and family, and the guidance of individuals like my spiritual mother, Apostle Andrea Zoe Legette. The Lord placed her in my life to unveil the truth of His glory. Her insights have profoundly impacted my understanding of my identity in Christ, and for that, I am immensely and eternally grateful, as she has been instrumental in unlocking many eternal truths within me.

I want to express heartfelt thanks to everyone who contributed to this journey—my husband for his unwavering support, my children for being my sounding boards and my encouragement to pursue a life different from what I was accustomed to, and my friends for their encouragement and wisdom. Your presence has been a source of strength that has fueled my passion for storytelling.

As you read these pages, I hope you find inspiration to reflect on your own life and the relationships that have shaped you. Each of us has a story to tell, and it is my hope that this book encourages you to embrace yours with courage and authenticity.

Thank you for joining me on this journey of discovering our identity in Christ Jesus.

About the Author

Jacqueline Hardin-Gautier is a minister of reconciliation to Christ Jesus, with a heartfelt desire to bring that which is out of order into order. At 43, she is a devoted mother of three and a proud grandmother of three grandchildren, cherishing the joy they bring to her life. Above all, Jacqueline is absolutely crazy about Jesus, who has become the affection and reason for everything she does.

As the founder of P139 Services LLC, Jacqueline operates a life coaching business, empowering individuals to discover their true identity and purpose. With a heart for service, Jacqueline navigates her role as a probation officer with compassion and purpose, supporting individuals within the criminal justice system during the challenging situations they have found themselves in. Jacqueline also participates in various volunteer efforts, furthering her commitment to helping others.

Jacqueline shares her insights and experiences on her blog, which she operates under the pen name P139 Girl. Through her writing, she creates a space for reflection and encouragement, drawing inspiration from Scripture and incorporating biblical truths into her coaching approach. Her poetry is a powerful testament to her faith, exploring themes of resilience, healing, and divine purpose, inspiring readers to embrace their unique journeys.

Family is central to Jacqueline's life, and she treasures the time spent with her loved ones. In her free time, she enjoys reading and writing, which allow her to express herself and connect with others.

Looking ahead, Jacqueline aims to deepen her ministry, expand her life coaching business, and continue supporting those in need, all while nurturing her family and uplifting her community.

You can connect with me on:

- https://p139girl.life
- https://p139services.com